# DOLPHINS

# FRESHWATER DOLPHINS

## JOHN F. PREVOST
### ABDO & Daughters

Published by Abdo & Daughters, 4940 Viking Drive, Suite 622, Edina, Minnesota 55435.

Library bound edition distributed by Rockbottom Books, Pentagon Tower, P.O. Box 36036, Minneapolis, Minnesota 55435.

Printed in the United States.

Cover Photo credit: Peter Arnold, Inc.

Interior Photo credits: Peter Arnold, Inc.

**Edited by Bob Italia**

**Library of Congress Cataloging-in-Publication Data**

Prevost, John F.
    Freshwater dolphins / by John F. Prevost.
        p. cm. — (Dolphins)
    Includes bibliographical references (p.23) and Index.
    ISBN 1-56239-492-4
1. River dolphins—Juvenile literature. [1. River dolphins. 2. Dolphins.] I. Title. II .
Series: Prevost, John F. Dolphins.
QL737.C436P74  1995
599.5'3—dc20                                    95-3315
                                                       CIP
                                                       AC

---

**ABOUT THE AUTHOR**

John Prevost is a marine biologist and diver who has been active in conservation and education issues for the past 18 years. Currently he is living inland and remains actively involved in freshwater and marine husbandry, conservation and education projects.

# Contents

# FRESHWATER DOLPHINS AND FAMILY

Freshwater dolphins live in rivers and **estuaries**. Because they are **mammals**, they breathe air with lungs, have hair when born, are **warm blooded**, and make milk for their babies. Unlike saltwater dolphins, freshwater dolphins live in fresh water.

There are 5 different freshwater dolphin **species**. All are mysterious and hard to study. Their sea cousins are the bottlenose dolphins, killer whales, and white-sided dolphins.

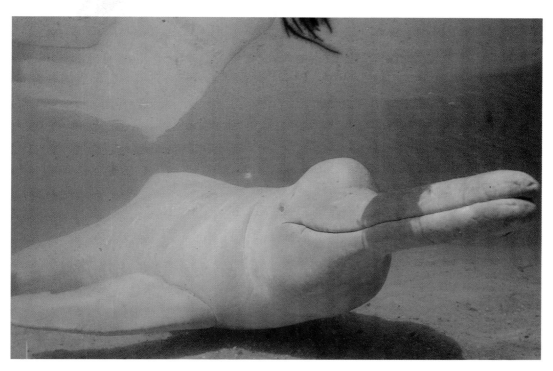

*The Amazon River dolphin is a freshwater mammal.*

# SIZE, SHAPE
# AND COLOR

The smallest freshwater dolphin is the 5-foot-long (1.5-meter-long) La Plata River dolphin. The largest is the 10-foot-long (3-meter-long) Amazon River dolphin.

Freshwater dolphins are not slim like their saltwater cousins. Their broad **flippers** bend and are paddle-shaped. Their snouts are up to 2 feet (60 cm) long.

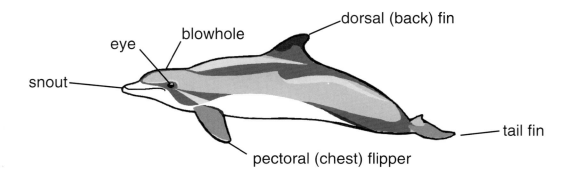

*Most dolphins share the same features.*

*The tail and flippers of the freshwater dolphin
are broad and flat.*

Freshwater dolphins' heads are large and round. Their necks can bend, and their stocky bodies are pink, blue, gray or white. La Plata River dolphins may also be light brown.

# WHERE THEY LIVE

Freshwater dolphins are found in South America and Asia. Most live only in fresh water. The La Plata River dolphins are the only freshwater dolphin also found in cloudy and sea waters. Freshwater dolphins avoid fast-moving water and are slow swimmers. They are also called river dolphins because they are usually found in rivers.

There are 5 freshwater dolphin **species**. Each is found in different **tropical** river systems. The Ganges River dolphin is found in western India, Bangladesh and Nepal. The Indus River dolphin is found in Pakistan. Both of

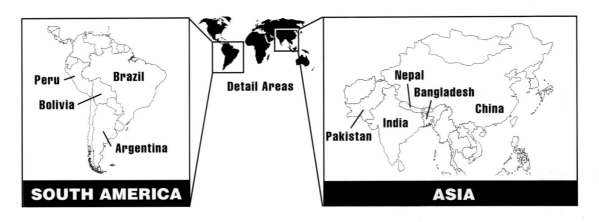

*The Ganges River dolphin.*

these dolphins are very similar but are separated by their different river systems.

The Chinese River dolphin is found in China's Yangtze River and some connected lakes. The Amazon River dolphin is found in Argentina, Bolivia, Brazil, and Peru. The La Plata River dolphin is found in Argentina and Brazil.

# SENSES

Freshwater dolphins and humans have 4 of the same senses. Most river water is dark and cloudy. So most freshwater dolphins cannot see well. To find **prey**, they use their hearing.

Like other dolphins, freshwater dolphins use **echolocation**. By making a series of clicks and whistles, these animals can "see" underwater by listening to the returning echoes.

Freshwater dolphins are **social** animals. They often touch each other to show feelings.

Scientists believe that dolphins can taste, but they do not know how well. Dolphins do not have a sense of smell.

# HOW ECHOLOCATION WORKS

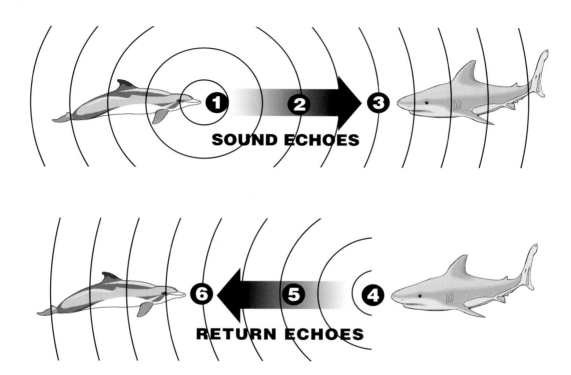

The dolphin sends out sound echoes (1). These echoes travel in all directions through the water (2). The sound echoes reach an object in the dolphin's path (3), then bounce off it (4). The return echoes travel through the water (5) and reach the dolphin (6). These echoes let the dolphin know where the object is, how large it is, and how fast it is moving.

# DEFENSE

Adult freshwater dolphins have no known natural enemies. Man is their only threat. These dolphins are rarely hunted for food. But they are found in areas where people are fishing, farming and forming industry. Some are killed when they are tangled in nets and drown.

Freshwater dolphins do not **migrate** out of their rivers. They follow **seasonal** flooding of the rivers in which they live. Dams that block their movement and low water levels are **hazards**.

Freshwater dolphins are shy. They avoid boats and people. But a polluted river is something they cannot escape.

**Freshwater dolphins are found in areas where people fish and farm. This is an Amazon River dolphin.**

# FOOD

Freshwater dolphins **prey** on different lake and river animals. Mostly they eat fish. With a long **snout** and bendable neck, river dolphins can easily grab fish. Long, thin, pointy teeth allow them to hold onto their prey.

Amazon River dolphins have special rear teeth that help crush heavily scaled fish. The Ganges and Indus River dolphins will also eat clams, **mussels**, and small shellfish. La Plata River dolphins travel into the Atlantic Ocean to feed on **squid**, octopus and shrimp.

Freshwater dolphins are **social** animals that will travel and hunt in **pods**. By using **echolocation**, they can find food in the cloudiest water.  By **communicating** with each other, they organize the hunt and trap schooling fish against riverbanks.

*Freshwater dolphins have long, thin, pointy teeth that allow them to hold onto their prey.*

# BABIES

A baby river dolphin is called a **calf**. At birth a calf is 22 to 29 inches (56 to 75 cm) long. Like other **mammals,** the mother makes milk for her calf.

Freshwater dolphins will **nurse** for one year. During that time, the mother protects and cares for the calf. Because the calves are small, large fish and **crocodilians** may attack them.

*A young Amazon River dolphin.*

# FRESHWATER DOLPHIN FACTS

**Scientific Name:**

Amazon River dolphin: *Inia geoffrensis*

Chinese River dolphin: *Lipotes vexillifer*

Ganges River dolphin: *Platanista gangetica*

Indus River dolphin: *P. minor*

La Plata River dolphin: *Pontoporia blainvillei*

**Average Size:** 7.5 feet (2.2 meters)
La Plata River dolphin is the smallest at 5 feet (1.5 meters).
Amazon River dolphin is the largest at 10 feet (3 meters).

**Where They're Found:** In a few river systems in Asia and South America.

*The freshwater dolphin.*

# GLOSSARY

**CALF** - A baby dolphin.

**COMMUNICATION** (kuh-mew-nih-KAY-shun) - To share or express feelings.

**CROCODILIANS** (krah-kuh-DILL-ee-unz) - Large reptiles with a long body, four short legs, thick skin, pointed snout, and a long tail.

**ECHOLOCATION** (ek-oh-low-KAY-shun) - The use of sound waves to locate objects.

**ESTUARY** (ES-tew-air-ee) - The mouth of a river where the current meets the sea.

**FLIPPERS** - The forelimbs of a sea mammal.

**HAZARD** - Something that is dangerous.

**MAMMAL** - A class of animals, including humans, that have hair and feed their young milk.

**MIGRATE** - To pass periodically from place to place.

**MUSSELS** - A water animal that has two hinged parts to its shell. Mussels look like clams.

**NURSE** - To feed a baby from its mother's breast.

**POD** - A group of sea mammals.

**PREDATOR** (PRED-uh-ter) - An animal that eats other animals.

**PREY** - Animals that are eaten by other animals.

**SEASONAL** (SEE-zun-ul) - Having to do with seasons.

**SNOUT** - The part of the animal's head that projects forward and includes the nose, mouth, and jaws.

**SOCIAL** (SOE-shull) - Living in organized groups.

**SPECIES** (SPEE-seas) - A plant or animal belonging to a particular classification.

**SQUID** - A group of marine animals related to the octopus that have a sleek shape and at least ten arms.

**TROPICAL** (TRAH-pih-kull) - The part of the Earth near the equator where the oceans are very warm.

**WARM-BLOODED** - An animal whose body temperature remains the same and warmer than the outside air or water temperature.

# Index

# BIBLIOGRAPHY

Cousteau, Jacques-Yves. *The Whale, Mighty Monarch of the Sea.* N.Y.: Doubleday, 1972.

Dozier, Thomas A. *Whales and Other Sea Mammals.* Time-Life Films, 1977.

Leatherwood, Stephen. *The Sierra Club Handbook of Whales and Dolphins.* San Francisco, California: Sierra Club Books, 1983.

Minasian, Stanley M. *The World's Whales.* Washington, D.C.: Smithsonian Books, 1984.

Ridgway, Sam H., ed. *Mammals of the Sea.* Springfield, Illinois: Charles C. Thomas Publisher, 1972.